The Showman

Kirsten Anderson

STECK-VAUGHN
ELEMENTARY · SECONDARY · ADULT · LIBRARY

A Harcourt Company

www.steck-vaughn.com

Photography: Cover ©Courtesy The Barnum Museum, Bridgeport, CT; Cover ©Courtesy of the Bridgeport Public Library; p.iv ©Photo Edit; p.2 ©Courtesy The Barnum Museum; p.4 ©Courtesy of the Bridgeport Public Library; p.6 ©Courtesy of the Bridgeport Public Library; p.7 ©Courtesy The Barnum Museum; p.9 ©Courtesy of the Bridgeport Public Library; p.11 ©Courtesy The Barnum Museum; p.13 ©Francis G. Mayer/CORBIS; p.14 ©S. Michael Bisceglie/Animals Animals; p.16 ©Bettmann/CORBIS; p.18(a,b) ©Courtesy The Barnum Museum; p.23 ©Courtesy The Barnum Museum.

Additional images by Steck-Vaughn Collection.

Contents

Chapter One

A Star Is Born

It's Spring, and the Circus Is Here!

New York, New York, 2002—It must be spring. The circus is in town again.

The Barnum & Bailey Circus has been around for more than 130 years. The shows used to take place in tents. Now they are **performed** indoors. Today you'll see fancy light shows. Of course, animals and people still do tricks. Sometimes there are **sideshows**. You can see the world's strongest man pull a truck. You may get to watch a man eat fire!

P. T. Barnum would have liked this circus. He always loved a good show. In fact, nobody put on a better show than P. T. Barnum.

Small Boy Likes Big Joke

Bethel, Connecticut, 1821–
P. T. Barnum thought he was the richest 11-year-old boy in town until yesterday.

P. T.'s grandfather gave him Ivy Island when he was born on July 5, 1810. P. T.'s family always told him how lucky he was. Neighbors said that Ivy Island was one of the best farms in Connecticut.

P. T. Barnum always liked a good joke.

P. T. had never seen his island. Finally, his family agreed that he should see it. P. T. was in for a surprise.

Yesterday, P. T. explored Ivy Island. It was not a fun adventure. P. T. stumbled into a **swamp** and stepped on a bee's nest. Then a snake came after him. Ivy Island was a terrible place.

Young P. T. knows that he was tricked, but he says that he always likes a good joke. P. T. tells us that his grandfather is more fun than anyone he knows. One day, P. T. hopes to be just like him.

Barnum's 160-Year-Old Woman

New York, New York, 1835—Mr. P. T. Barnum has opened a show here in New York City. People can't wait to meet the 160-year-old woman in his show. How in the world did Barnum find her?

Mr. Barnum was working in his store one day last summer. A friend stopped by to visit. He described a show that he wanted to sell. The show starred a 160-year-old woman. Barnum was interested. He decided to go meet Joice Heth, the 160-year-old woman.

Barnum described Miss Heth as a tiny lady. Her face looked as rough and dry as an elephant's. The old lady could barely move. She also had no teeth, and she couldn't see.

Miss Heth **claimed** that she had taken care of George Washington when he was a boy. She told Barnum stories about "dear little George." Miss Heth also showed Barnum a **receipt** from 1727. The receipt showed that George Washington's father had bought her to be a slave. ⚡

Barnum was pleased by Miss Heth, so he bought the show. He hung up **posters** on the streets. Soon crowds were lining up to see her.

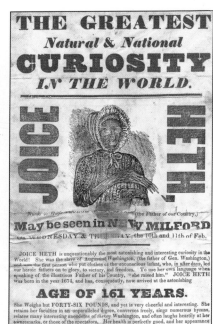

THE GREATEST
Natural & National
CURIOSITY
IN THE WORLD.

JOICE HETH

May be seen in NEW MILFORD
On WEDNESDAY & THURSDAY, the 10th and 11th of Feb.

JOICE HETH is unquestionably the most astonishing and interesting curiosity in the World! She was the slave of Augustine Washington, (the father of Gen. Washington,) and was the first person who put clothes on the unconscious infant, who, in after days, led our heroic fathers on to glory, to victory, and freedom. To use her own language when speaking of the illustrious Father of his Country, "she raised him." JOICE HETH was born in the year 1674, and has, consequently, now arrived at the astonishing

AGE OF 161 YEARS.

She weighs but FORTY-SIX POUNDS, and yet is very cheerful and interesting. She retains her faculties in an unparalleled degree, converses freely, sings numerous hymns, relates many interesting anecdotes of *the* boy Washington, and often laughs heartily at her own remarks, or those of the spectators. Her health is perfectly good, and her appearance very neat. She is a baptist and takes great pleasure in conversing with ministers and religious persons. The appearance of this marvellous relic of antiquity strikes the beholder with amazement, and convinces him that he now sees resting on the oldest specimen of mortality they ever before beheld. Original, authentic, and indisputable documents accompany her on her journeys, however improbable, positive mention of her age, &c. &c., they expect the person she is represented.

The most eminent physicians and intelligent men in Cincinnati, Philadelphia, New York, Boston, and other places, have examined this *living skeleton* and the documents accompanying her, and all, *invariably,* pronounce her to be, as represented, 161 years of age!

A female is in constant attendance, and will give every attention to the ladies who visit this relic of by-gone ages.

She has been visited in Philadelphia, New-York, Boston, &c., by more than TWENTY THOUSAND Ladies and Gentlemen, within the last three months.

Hours of Exhibition, from 9 A. M. to 1 P. M. and from 3 to 5, and 6½ to 10 P. M.

ADMITTANCE 25 Cents. CHILDREN HALF-PRICE.

Printed by J. BOOTH & SON, 147, Fulton-st N. Y.

When Barnum put up posters like this one, people lined up to see Joice Heth.

The crowds keep coming. Barnum says he loves entertaining them. Ah, what a life!

The Truth About the 161-Year-Old Woman

Philadelphia, Pennsylvania, Feb. 19, 1836– Joice Heth died today. Doctors have **examined** her body. They say that she was only about 80 years old. Her insides were in such good shape that she couldn't have been 161!

When P. T. Barnum learned the news, he seemed surprised. He said that he truly believed that Joice Heth was 161. Barnum claimed that he had been tricked. He pointed to his receipt from 1727. Did Barnum trick everyone, or did Barnum's friend trick him?

If Barnum were playing a trick, we would not be surprised. A few months ago, Barnum took Miss Heth to Boston. A **rumor** started there that she was a machine, not a person. It was said that a man hid during the shows and spoke for the machine. Before this rumor started, ticket sales were low. Some people think that Barnum himself started the rumor to **improve** sales.

GREAT ATTRACTION
JUST ARRIVED AT HINGHAM.
FOR A SHORT TIME ONLY.
JOICE HETH,
NURSE TO
Gen. George Washington,

(The father of our country,) who has arrived at the astonishing age of **161** years! will be seen at HINGHAM for a SHORT TIME ONLY, as she is to fill other engagements very soon.

JOICE HETH is unquestionably the most astonishing and interesting curiosity in the World! She was the slave of Augustine Washington, (the father of Gen. Washington,) and was the first person who put clothes on the unconscious infant who in after days led our heroic fathers on to glory, to victory and freedom. To use her own language when speaking of the illustrious Father of his country, "she raised him." JOICE HETH was born in the Island of Madagascar, on the Coast of Africa, in the year 1674 and has consequently now arrived at the astonishing

Age of 161 Years!

She weighs but forty-six pounds, and yet is very cheerful and interesting. She retains her faculties in an unparalleled degree, converses freely, sings numerous hymns, relates many interesting anecdotes of the boy Washington, the red coats, &c. and often laughs heartily at her own remarks, or those of the spectators. Her health is perfectly good, and her appearance very neat. She was baptized in the Potomac river and received into the Baptist Church 116 years ago, and takes great pleasure in conversing with Ministers and religious persons. The appearance of this marvellous relic of antiquity strikes the beholder with amazement, and convinces him that his eyes are resting on the oldest specimen of mortality they ever before beheld. Original, authentic and indisputable documents prove however astonishing the fact may appear, JOICE HETH is in every respect the person she is represented.

The most eminent physicians and intelligent men in Cincinnati, Philadelphia, New-York, Boston and many other places have examined this *living skeleton* and the documents accompanying her, and all *invariably* pronounce her to be as represented 161 *years of age!* Indeed it is impossible for any person, however incredulous, to visit her without astonishment and the most perfect satisfaction that she is as old as represented.

☞ A female is in continual attendance, and will give every attention to the ladies who visit this relic of by gone ages.

She was visited at Niblo's Garden New York, by *ten thousand persons* in two weeks.———Hours of exhibition from 9 A. M to 1 P. M. and from 3 to 6 and from 7 to 9 P. M.—Admittance 25 cents—Children 12½ cents.

☞ For further particulars, see newspapers of the day.   ☞ Over

> **Barnum used many posters to bring people to his shows.**

Some people believe that Barnum made up Joice Heth's story. They think that he lied about the receipt. Barnum still claims that he never lied.

What is the truth? We may never know. But one thing is certain. People paid money for this big, bad **hoax**. Barnum should have learned the truth about Joice Heth before he opened his show.

Chapter Two

The American Museum

American Museum Has New Owner

New York, New York, 1842–The American Museum in New York City will soon open again. We spoke to Francis Olmsted, the first owner. He said that he sold the **museum** to Mr. P. T. Barnum. Barnum has little money but owns three pieces of land. One of them, Ivy Island, is said to be very nice.

Barnum filled his American Museum with exciting exhibits.

Olmsted gave Barnum $2,000 **credit** for the land. Barnum still owes $10,000 for the museum, but Barnum is a land owner. A man like that can surely be **trusted** to pay.

Barnum claims that he plans to make the museum bigger and better. But it will be difficult to improve the museum without much money. Good luck, Mr. Barnum! We'll be watching for news of great changes.

Amazing Sights at the American Museum

New York, New York, 1842–When Mr. P. T. Barnum bought the American Museum, he claimed that he would improve it. Well, it seems that he has done so. We hear that the museum has many interesting **exhibits**. We decided to go and see them for ourselves.

Mr. Barnum has worked hard to get people to come to his museum. On our way there, we saw posters about it everywhere.

Inside the museum, we saw amazing things. There are paintings and other art. The museum

People came to Barnum's museum to see his amazing exhibits, such as this hairy family.

is also full of odd objects. You will see trick mirrors like those at a carnival. You'll jump away from scary **mummies**. Be careful when you go around corners!

The museum also has many animals. Don't miss the "Happy Family." This is a cage filled with trained animals. The cats don't eat the mice, and the owls don't eat the rabbits!

Another exhibit is a cow with two heads. It is a strange-looking **creature**. Our favorite exhibit is the dog that plays cards. It would be nice to have a dog like that at home!

There are also many interesting people on exhibit. We saw a 20-year-old man who is only three feet tall! An eight-foot-tall giant **towers over** him. Another man is so thin, you can see right through him!

All in all, we passed an interesting day at Mr. Barnum's American Museum. We believe it is worth a visit.

Strange Creature Sighted in Philadelphia!

New York, New York, 1842–Dr. J. Griffin has all of Philadelphia talking. He has bought a **mermaid**. Dr. Griffin says that it is from the Feejee (Fiji) Islands. News **reporters** have seen the mermaid and believe that it is real.

P. T. Barnum has asked Dr. Griffin to bring the mermaid to New York City. Barnum would like to show the mermaid at his museum.

Sadly, the doctor has **refused**. We hope that he changes his mind.

Feejee Mermaid Not Real

New York, New York, 1842–
The Feejee Mermaid has been on exhibit at Barnum's museum for one month. Posters and newspaper **ads** showed a pretty woman with a fish tail. But the mermaid isn't pretty. It's an ugly, dried-up thing.

It turns out that the mermaid is not from the Feejee Islands. It was made in Japan from a monkey's head and the tail of a fish. P. T. Barnum knew all along that this was a **fake**!

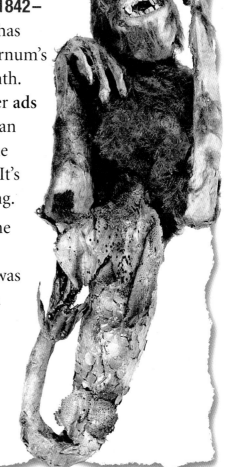

The Feejee (Fiji) mermaid was a hoax.

The man called Dr. Griffin is a **fraud**. His real name is Levi Lyman. He and Barnum made up the mermaid story to make money.

Most people don't seem to mind that the mermaid is a fake. They say that it is still a good show. Barnum agrees. He claims that people got their money's worth.

Barnum should be **ashamed** for tricking so many people. Instead, he plans to take the mermaid on tour next week. Save your money, America. Don't spend it to see a fake.

The Wild West Is Not So Wild

New York, New York, 1843—For the past few weeks, newspapers have shown ads for a **buffalo** hunt in Hoboken, New Jersey. The ads claimed that a hunter would chase big buffalo across a field. It would be just like a real buffalo hunt in the Wild West. Best of all, the show would be free!

People expected to see a buffalo hunt such as this one.

The first people to see the show had quite a surprise. The buffalo weren't big, as the ads had claimed. They were just babies. When the buffalo hunter came onto the field, the buffalo didn't **stampede**. Instead, they all stood together and wouldn't move. They looked so funny that the **audience** began to laugh. The buffalo were scared by the noise and ran into a swamp!

We talked to a few people who saw the show. Were they angry that they had been tricked? Not at all, they said. They cheered for whoever had planned such a funny show.

One man laughed and said that P. T. Barnum must have planned the show.

People didn't mind seeing baby buffalo such as this one. After all, the show was free.

A woman told us that the show had been a good joke. Another woman said that she had fun. Anyway, it was a nice day to be outdoors, she added.

It makes you wonder. Would these people have liked the joke as much if it had rained?

Chapter Three

Losing Some, Winning More

Little Tom Thumb Gets a Big Hand

New York, New York, 1844—This news just came in from London. Tom Thumb has met the Queen!

Barnum hired Thumb last year to entertain at his museum. Barnum claimed that Thumb was 11 years old, but many people said that he was only four. Whatever his real age, Thumb was tiny. He stood just two feet tall and **weighed** only 16 pounds!

Barnum taught Thumb to perform songs and jokes for shows at the American Museum. Thumb was a big **success**. Barnum felt sure that Thumb would do well in England, too. So the two sailed to England in January.

P. T. Barnum and Tom Thumb became good friends.

When they **arrived** in England, Barnum set up a show for young Queen Victoria. Tom Thumb **charmed** the Queen with songs and dances. The show made him famous. Now all of England wants to see him perform.

Good luck in England, Tom Thumb. America misses you, so hurry home soon.

Americans Are Crazy About Jenny Lind

New York, New York, 1850—Jenny Lind has won the hearts of Americans. But a few months ago, no one even knew who she was.

Mr. P. T. Barnum of the American Museum brought the singer to New York. He had never heard her sing, but he knew that people in Europe loved her. He took a chance and brought her to America.

Weeks before Miss Lind arrived, Barnum placed ads in newspapers. He hired a reporter to write about Miss Lind. The stories said that Miss Lind was a **generous** woman. She gave most of her money to poor or sick people.

Mr. Barnum sure is smart. Soon Jenny Lind chairs, hats, and dolls were for sale all over the city. Miss Lind was famous before she arrived.

Mr. Barnum can sell anything. Once, he hired **musicians** to play outside his museum. They sounded terrible! People entered the museum just to get away from the noise.

M'lle Jenny Lind's

GRAND CONCERT.

ADMIT ONE.   *P.T. Barnum*

Van Norden & American, Printers, 60 D Slam street, New York

**Barnum made sure that Jenny Lind was well known
even before she arrived in the United States.**

But Miss Lind is not a trick. A crowd of five thousand people came to her first show. Miss Lind charmed everyone with her wonderful voice. ♪

Few people can sing as well as Jenny Lind. P. T. Barnum has shown us that she is a fine person, too.

Barnum's American Museum Lost to Fire

New York, New York, 1865—Mr. P. T. Barnum's American Museum has burned down. Barnum says that he will build a new museum soon.

A few months ago, someone asked Barnum why he showed such silly exhibits. His answer was, "Men, women, and children cannot always be serious." He claimed that a museum should teach things, but it should also be fun.

Mr. Barnum's idea of fun is wrong. His museum had no real worth. Paintings shouldn't be shown with giants. Mermaids don't belong with mummies. Barnum **treated** art like it was a joke. ♪

Mr. Barnum only cared about making money. He treated his customers like fools. One time, he put up signs in his museum. These signs said **EGRESS**. People followed the signs, sure that they would see a new kind of animal. Instead, the signs led them out the **exit** door. Barnum claimed that the sign kept the crowd moving and the museum from getting too full. But was that a kind way to treat his customers?

Some people thought Barnum treated his customers like fools. Most people enjoyed his shows very much.

Barnum always claimed that he wanted to entertain people. But a museum is not a circus. Barnum should keep this in mind if he opens another museum.

Chapter Four

Barnum Leaves Us with a Circus

Barnum Makes a Comeback

New York, New York, 1872–P. T. Barnum, that famous **showman**, is back with a new show. He is now the owner of a circus. No one has ever seen a circus like this. The tents hold twenty thousand people. Bears and elephants dance. Monkeys ride in camel races. There's even a goat that rides a horse. The goat leaps through hoops, then lands on the horse's back!

Of course, there are also wonderful sideshows. The Palestine Giant and Admiral Dot are a popular act. The eight-foot-tall giant can hold tiny Mr. Dot in his hand!

Audiences say that they like Barnum's circus. This is no surprise to us. P. T. Barnum always puts on a good show. ⚡

Famous Showman Dies

Bridgeport, Connecticut, 1891–P. T. Barnum died yesterday at his home here in Bridgeport. Mr. Barnum was 81 years old. During his life, he became one of the most famous people in America.

Barnum knew that people wanted to get their money's worth from a show. So, he got people's **attention** and made them believe his shows were the best. He put ads in newspapers and hung posters. He made up stories and rumors.

Barnum showed America amazing things. Some were real, and some were not. Barnum's shows made us think and wonder, and he always entertained us. He really was the greatest showman on Earth. ⚡

We'll miss you, Mr. Barnum. We'll always think of you when the circus comes to town.

Though he was known as the World's Greatest Showman, P. T. Barnum was not in any of his own shows.

Glossary

ads (ADZ) *noun* Ads are written or spoken words that are used to make people want to buy or see something.

arrived (uh RYVD) *verb* Arrived means came to a place.

ashamed (uh SHAYMD) *adjective* To be ashamed is to feel bad for something that you did.

attention (uh TEHN shuhn) *noun* Attention is the act of watching or keeping your mind on a person or a thing.

audience (AW dee uhns) *noun* An audience is people who watch a show.

buffalo (BUF uh loh) *adjective* Buffalo means having to do with the large, furry brown animal that is like a cow and is called a buffalo.

charmed (CHAHRMD) *verb* Charmed means pleased someone by saying or doing something very nice.

claimed (KLAYMD) *verb* Claimed means said something that you believed was true or wanted others to believe.

creature (KREE chuhr) *noun* A creature is a living thing, such as an animal.

credit (KREHD iht) *noun* Credit is money taken out of an amount a person owes.

egress (EE grehs) *noun* An egress is a way that leads outside. It is another word for exit.

examined (ehg ZAM uhnd) *verb* Examined means looked at something very carefully.

exhibits (ehg ZIHB ihts) *noun* Exhibits are objects or animals seen at museums or in zoos.

exit (EHG ziht) *adjective* An exit door is a door that leads outside.

fake (FAYK) *noun* A fake is something that is not what it looks like or is said to be.

fraud (FRAWD) *noun* A fraud is a person who tricks other people by pretending to be someone else.

generous (JEHN uhr uhs) *adjective* To be generous is to be helpful or to share what you have with others.

hoax (HOHKS) *noun* A hoax is a trick or mean joke.

improve (ihm PROOV) *verb* To improve means to make something better than it was before.

mermaid (MUHR mayd) *noun* A mermaid is a sea animal that is not real. It has the body of a woman and the tail of a fish.

mummies (MUM eez) *noun* Mummies are dead bodies that are wrapped in cloth.

museum (myoo ZEE uhm) *noun* A museum is a building that shows art objects, science objects, and objects from the past.

musicians (myoo ZIHSH uhnz) *noun* Musicians are people who play music.

performed (puhr FAWRMD) *adjective* To be performed means to be put on, as in an act or show.

posters (POHS tuhrz) *noun* Posters are big pieces of paper covered by pictures and words.

receipt (ree SEET) *noun* A receipt is a piece of paper that you get when you buy something.

refused (rih FYOOZD) *verb* Refused means a person was asked to do something and said no.

reporters (rih PAWRT uhrz) *noun* Reporters are people who tell or write about the news.

rumor (ROO muhr) *noun* A rumor is a story told as news and passed from person to person. A rumor may or may not be true.

showman (SHOH muhn) *noun* A showman is a man who works with circus people, singers, actors, or dancers.

sideshows (SYD shohz) *noun* Sideshows are circus shows that are not in the main tent.

stampede (stam PEED) *verb* To stampede is to run together in a group.

success (suhk SEHS) *noun* A success is a person who becomes very popular or makes a lot of money.

swamp (SWAHMP) *noun* A swamp is a piece of wet land that is full of mud, water, and plants.

towers over (TOW uhrz OH vuhr) *verb* Towers over means stands taller than another person or thing.

treated (TREET uhd) *verb* Treated means acted a certain way toward a person or a thing.

trusted (TRUST uhd) *adjective* Someone who is trusted can be expected to do what they say they will do.

weighed (WAYD) *verb* Weighed means measured a certain number of pounds.

Index